Buried Alive

Dead Men Do Talk!

Buried Alive

Dead Men Do Talk!

By: Halim A. Flowers

Struggle Against The Odds Publications

Dedication

To my Aunt Ruth
who gave me books when everyone
else gave me toys!

CONTENTS

The Wake

THE SUPERIOR COURT OF THE DISTRICT
OF COLOMBIA CRIMINAL DIVISION

Criminal Action
Volume I of I
July 1998
Washington, D.C

The above-entitled came on for a Sentencing Hearing Proceeding **SOME PARTS OF THIS TRANSCRIPT WAS ALTERED AND NAMES WERE REMOVED.** THE TRANSCIPT REPRESENTED *SOME* OF THE PRODUCT OF AN OFFICIAL REPORTER, ENGAGED BY THE COURT.

APPEARANCES:
On behalf of the Government:

HERRING, Esquire
Assistant United States Attorney

On behalf of the Defendant:
ROBERTS, Esquire
Washington, D.C.

P RO C E E D I N G S

THE DEPUTY CLERK: On Your Honor's sentencing calendar, the United State versus Halim Flowers.

ATTORNEY FOR THE DEFENDANT: Good morning, Your Honor. Attorney for the Defendant: Halim Flowers.

ASSISTANT ATTORNEY: Good morning, Your Honor. For the record, Albert Herring for the United States.

THE DEPUTY CLERK: Your Honor, the deputies need a couple of minutes to get Mr. Flowers.

ATTORNEY FOR THE DEFENDANT: Mr. Flowers is present.

THE COURT: Mr. Flowers is present. This matter is before the court for sentencing, and I've had an opportunity to read the materials that have been submitted. A copy of the letter from the family which has been seen by counsel for Mr. Flowers.

Attorney for the Defendant, you've seen it?

ATTORNEY FOR THE DEFENDANT: Yes. Yes, Your Honor. I was just provided a copy this morning and reviewed it and Mr. Flowers had an opportunity to review it as well.

THE COURT: Okay. I'll hear the parties allocution.

ATTORNEY FOR THE DEFENDANT: Thank you, Your Honor.

Your Honor, with respect to the presentence report, there are no accuracies or material inaccuracies

THE COURT: Okay.

ATTORNEY FOR THE DEFENDANT: I won't obviously comment on the verdict in this case. Mr. Flowers and I, while disappointed, accept that the jury has spoken with regard to the proof in this case. And given that Mr. Flowers does intend to appeal his convictions, I won't go further than that.

I will just say a couple of things, Your Honor. We are both, that is Mr. Flowers and I are both mindful of what the maximum possible penalty that this Court can impose in this case is, and it's clear to say frightening.

Mr. Flowers, and I'll use my - - Mister - - as the Court is aware is seventeen year old, and he's indeed a younger than - - I began practicing law before he was born and this is probably, at least for me personally, one of the more difficult places I can find myself as a defense attorney.

When standing with someone who is before the court facing a minimum possible sentence which is far in excess the number of years he has even lived, I only wish that whatever was available could have been made available to Mr. Flowers when he was in the juvenile system. It may have had some impact on - - on - - on his future.

He is not someone who is - - who is stupid. In fact, what is quite impressive about Mr. Flowers is he is among the brighter clients I have of any age. He's a bright young man who I note that the court needs to - - assume we have to throw away.

He does indeed have a very, very supportive family. Indeed, many members of that family are here and they've been here throughout these proceedings.

What I guess I would like to impress upon the Court is that I think that the thirty years, the mandatory that the court must impose in this case, is far more than is necessary in order to address each of the things that the Court will understandably will address in imposing a sentence, clearly being locked away for thirty years is a long time, and that will clearly punish Mr. Flowers. But I don't think that we have to decide that he has to die in prison.

Forty-seven is not as old as it sounds. I know because I am rapidly approaching that age. And given what I think Mr. Flowers is capable of being, I would just submit to the Court that the Court need not in this case go beyond the mandatory minimum.

I would point that even under the Government's theory Mr. Flowers was not the shooter in this case. And while obviously he has been found guilty as an aider and abetter, to the extent that the Court can make some distinction between his conduct and the conduct of the co-defendant, he is not the shooter.

Again, if we were talking about a term of incarceration of a mere ten years, that's hard to say, or a mere fifteen years, then I probably would not have much of an argument to make to make to the Court. But I can't imagine why thirty years is not sufficient punishment given the facts of this case and giving how young he is.

So my request on Mr. Flowers' behalf is that the Court impose no more than the mandatory minimum thirty years to life.

THE COURT: Thank you. Mr. Herring

ASSISTANT ATTORNEY: Thank you, Your Honor.

Your Honor, it may sound somewhat strange to hear me use the terminology "bare minimum" when were talking about the imposition of a mandatory minimum sentence of thirty year

incarceration, but the reality is what defense counsel is asking you
to impose in this case is the bare minimum that the law requires
that you impose. Not that you impose in an exercise of your discre-
tion, but that you are required by law to impose.

And while I appreciate the significance of Attorney for the
Defendant ' comments about Mr. Flowers' youth, I simply cannot
endorse the defense's request that the Court impose no more than
the bare minimum in his case.

And I start with the proposition, Your Honor, that the Court
should consider that at the time Mr. Flowers should engage in two
series of criminal acts, and that is, in fact that we are talking about,
two series of criminal acts, albeit committed over the course of
one continuance transaction.

He was on probation having been adjudicated for assault while
intent to kill while armed. Not even on probation for a full year in
a case in which he had shot two other kids while they were on the
playground of a school. Not only was Mr. Flowers adjudicated for
that offense, but there was coupled with it the offense of carrying
the dangerous weapon that he used to shoot those people.

And then I think as the presentence report writer says it best
on page 10 of his presentence report when Mr. Flowers was frus-
trated in his effort to rob a man who had every right to hold onto
what he had earned, and as you can see from the VICITM family
THE VICITM was a man who has worked for a living to earn the
money he had.

Mr. Flowers displayed a brazenly ruthlessness an audacious
determination to meet out his own kind of justice to someone
who had the nerve to stand up and say no. And I think that when
you measure Mr. Flowers' contribution in the loss of this man's
life, because but for Mr. Flowers setting in motion the chain of
events which ultimately claimed his life, that man may very well be
alive today. The bare minimum simply is not sufficient.

I can't pretend that I believe Mr. Flowers should receive the
maximum period of incarceration available here because as
Attorney for the Defendant pointed out, he was not the shooter. But

I also believe that the Court should not ignore the fact that Mr. Flowers was the person who touched off the whole chain of events.

The Court should be mindful of the tremendous impact that the loss of this man's life has had on the family who has had to suffer continuing on in his absence.

I think the VICTIM sister points out quite eloquently that even though her brother is not with them in body he is still with them in heart and spirit, and they remember him in the light - - and remember him in the light of the contribution he made to their family, how he helped to provide for the household and how he was a good brother to them.

We ask, Your Honor, that in light of Mr. Flowers' criminal history, and it is a criminal history no matter how much we want to emphasize the fact that he is seventeen, he was a seventeen-year-old capable of knowing right and wrong and knowingly chose to do wrong having had the benefit of only a few months earlier being a chance, a second chance having done wrong, that you impose more than the bare minimum in this case and impose a sentence that allows Mr. Flowers to learn the lesson that the VICTIM sister herself points out, he should not be allowed to be released from prison without learning , and that is no matter how young you are, you are responsible for what you do and you stand accountable for it.

THE COURT: Okay. Mr. Flowers is there anything you would like to say before the court imposes sentence.

THE DEFENDANT: No, Sir.

THE COURT: Okay. For your family who is here to support you it's not an easy job for a judge to impose sentence on those who have been convicted of homicide offenses, particularly over the years and I've pasted the forty-seven year mark where I see those who have been convicted get younger and younger.

It startles me every year, the older I get the younger the young people who come before me are. And I remember seeing you during the course of the trial and if a group of citizens just came in and saw you they would be initially just shocked because you are so young, so young looking, and a young person.

And I don't know where you went wrong or the quote, unquote, the criminal justice system went wrong; our educational system went wrong, what happened that we couldn't reach you in the juvenile system after you were adjudicated with that other assault with intent to kill. Why couldn't we reach you so that you would understand how horrible that was and that you have to resist the life of guns, you know, and using guns and being so oblivious to the, you know, the horrors that guns cause in all of our lives, you know.

And I really think, and I struggle with this every Friday when I do these sentences. I really do think that because young people like yourself are so young when they get involved in these types of behaviors that simply don't have any sense of what it means. You know, it's very hard I'm sure, Mr. Flowers as much as you try to understand what it means to die, to not marry, to not have children, to go through disappointments. It's hard when you're seventeen to really understand what life is all about. Its ups and downs and taking a human life and what that means.

And I'm talking to you and I know it is difficult for you, and at this time you probably want to just hear Judge - - just tell me how much time I'm going to get. You know, the response that I hear a lot is what I can do about it now. It's over. He's dead, lets move on.

It's not that simple. I don't think you deserve the maximum consecutive sentences for every offense. I'm not going to impose that. You are not the shooter. You were the one that started this. But I also agree that the absolute minimum required by law is also not appropriate only because of the aggravating circumstances that you having a chance to back away from this.

I mean, there were two entries. There was an initial entry when you came in, the robbery didn't work out. You could have just left, but you came back again. And that's when the shooting took place.

I simply just can't say well, fine, that's all right, that's - - all should be concurrent. I just can't do that. It doesn't mean I have to give you the maximum sentence, and I'm not going to do that, but I will have to give you a consecutive with respect to the second entry.

(PARTS ALTERED)

The only consecutive sentence will be the second entry which will be ten to thirty years with a mandatory five. All other sentences are concurrent to each other.

Mr. Flowers, you have the right to appeal your convictions. You need to note your appeal timely, within thirty days. You have the right to an attorney on appeal. If you cannot afford one, one will be provided for you. If you don't note your appeal within thirty days you will lose your right to appeal.

Thank you very much.

*   *   *   *

(Proceedings concluded for the day.)

...So now that you have read my obituary!

Buried Alive

Dead Men Do Talk!

Sorry Mama for writing another book that will make you cry!

Magnum Opus

In a circle of hate
It may seem strange to love
To reach where you can no longer hold a grudge
It's deep
Because I even forgave my judge
It was a formidable challenge
Because my callous had mileage
I had to travel deep within myself
Just to remove the malice
The sword of peace to defeat the inner beast and savage
But I'm not claiming to be perfect
Like I can't eat from the forbidden fruit if I'm deceived
  by the serpent
Knowledge is born
I break life down to its most original form
Atoms consist of positives and negatives
I weather the storm
Just as the sun shines
It get cloudy sometimes
A mixture of joy and pain
I just throw on my mental Gortex and walk slow
  through the rain
I ain't going to run or use an umbrella
I'm a walk through it slow
And get a little bit wet
Cause without water
Life can't grow!

Mixed Emotions

Celia, a teenage slave girl, in June 1855 murdered her owner Robert
Newsome. Celia had become impregnated three times by her seventy
five year old owner sexually assaulting her. She told him that if he
attempted to rape her again that she would kill him, and she proved
that her word was bond when she sent him to his maker. The Missouri
trial judge and the Missouri Supreme Court refused to give the jury a
self defense instruction at Celia's trial. The jury convicted Celia of
murder and sentenced her to death. The judge delayed the execution
until the baby was born. After the birth of the child Celia was hanged.
This is a true story in Amerikan history. Justice Prevails! The Struggle
Continues…

What does the slave girl feel?
When she is impregnated with hate
And experiences the pain of birth
To have a baby fathered by rape
When she sees the newborn infant and starts to cry
Is it because she is happy or that she wants her child to die
If you could understand the language of her tears
You would hear the anguish and fears!

Walls of Captivity

This writing was inspired by prison walls and book "The Count of Monte Cristo" by Alexandre Dumas….

These walls are impregnated with tears
Waiting for its water to break
And secrete the pain of the tormented that it holds captive
Thinking for what reason has fate delegated it this horrid
      position
To smother the very dreams of deprived men and women
Imposing its structure from four enclosing corners
Enveloping the broken spirits
These walls are impregnated with tears
For they have felt the cold skin from the lifeless man hanging
      from the vent
They have been painted with the blood of the slain
Absorbed the curse of the insane
Felt the kicks from the vain
Heard the prayers of the oppressed when the gates of heaven
      opened for rain
These walls are impregnated with tears
For they know that even amongst the strongest they strike fear
Imagine if you were a grave for the living
These walls are impregnated with tears……

The Prince of Peace
The King of Sorrow

The eulogy of the condemned man buried alive inside of hell.

He wakes up in his grave
And looks in the mirror
His life turns a page
And his visions are clearer
He's been thrown in a cage
In the custody of sadists
A reflection of rage
Surrounded by madness
Casted to a dungeon as a juvenile
To be raised by the beast
But he grew to be a beautiful man-child
A Prince of Peace
The King of Sorrow
Who smiles at his tomorrows?
Even when hopes were shallow
And miracles could not be borrowed
A product of the gun and crack era
Mothers feel his pain
And spread their eye shadow
When they flood their faces with tears like rain
His chest is out
And his shoulders are square
Wisdom dwells on his mouth
And his judgments are fair
His captors hate
That he smiles at his fate

They tried to bury him alive
But he still screams "FREEDOM" at the gates
They isolated him to a cell
He succeeded where most have failed
To not be burned of his sanity
By the fires of his hell
The Prince of Peace
The King of Sorrow
They tried to bleach his thoughts with defeat
And bury his tomorrows
They shoveled dirt in his face
And prayed that he wouldn't resist
But he kept clawing at his grave
Until he saw daylight
And gave them the Clinched Fist!

My View

I wrote this poem in attempt to explain my position and view of being held captive by people who express more violence and physical aggression then the slaves that they keep Imprisoned.

Imagine a praying man in a position that denies him trust to
     love his Queen
Imagine a breathing King who is held caged by the resistance of
     living ghosts
Imagine a person who has lost the art of secreting tears
Imagine a world in where strangers become closer to you than
     family and your loved ones are
As distant as strangers
Imagine a wise man under the custody of sadist
Imagine if the only person you made love to was your hand
Imagine a man of love who feared to love
Imagine a man of trust who could not trust
Imagine one man against a superpower
Why waste the imagination?
I AM!

Abandoned Child

My view of how society gave me up for adoption to be nurtured by the hells of confinement.

I once used to be a normal person
Before they decided to hang me
Before I was angry
The world gave up on me
Said that I was too ugly for society to see
Now nobody but zombies get to see how beautiful I have grown
    to be
I've been outcasted
One of the children beneath the stairs
A monster
To be chained
Chained worser than anything that ever existed
See
I am the child that the world no longer wanted
Ever again
I once used to smile a lot
Before they buried that part of me
The part of me that made me human
The part of me that used to be able to cry
Before my soul went dry…

I Failed

We are easy to judge everyone harshly, but look in the mirror
    and smile with merciful forgiveness upon our ugliness
    as if our flaws don't exist.

This is the hardest thing for most to admit
All loved to be praised
But few employ self-criticism
It took a few years for me to realize
And once recognized
A few more years for me to admit
Mother I failed you
Father I failed you
Brother, Sister, Aunts, Uncles, Cousins, Grandparents, Family,
    Friends, Community, my people I failed you
I sacrificed my intellect for a drink, some smoke, chasing money
    and women, and an image
I failed everyone
More importantly myself
Sixteen with a life sentence
I failed miserably
I've been deemed a menace
Society has outcasted me for eternity
With that said
I now move forward
For I am not a failure
The failing is complete
I have nothing to lose but my chains
Nowhere to look but up
See a failure is content with his errors
The strong though fall

Fight their way up
I will walk with wise
And take my seat amongst the sages
But without my failings
How could I have become the man I am today?
I failed…

Cold World

I wrote this after thinking about Stevie Wonder's song "Rocket Love".

Foreigners invading distant land
Imposing liberation through missiles
Colonizers labeling natives as savage insurrectionist
Quislings praised as heroes
Suicide bombs
Single moms
Punctured o-zone layers
Ice caps crying
I'm trapped in this cold world
Former slaves sing Pariotic anthems for stolen lands and nations
Video "games" with guns and murder
Children kill in class
Police cuff five year old children
Parents are apprehended by the state for disciplining their
        offspring
Youth runs reckless
Elders paralyzed by fear
Wisdom and direction is lost
I'm trapped in this cold world
Confusion rampant where unity should exist
Crips and bloods
Sunni and Shi'ite
Man and woman searching for love in a loveless time
A lovely universe consumed with hate
The Human Genetic Blueprint made simple
But the explanation of love so difficult
Babies aborted
Babies in trash cans

Babies in bars
I'm trapped in this cold world
New crusades masquerade behind the disguise to Democracize
Bombs explode upon the soil for merely suggestions
Pre-emptive redemptions for crimes waiting to be committed
I only wanted peace amongst a people who preach
     self-destruction
Just wanted to love in a loveless time
Maybe a lovely moment in this lovely creation
This lovely universe
But I'm still trapped in this cold World!!!

Struggle of Life

This poem is inspired by the title of Talib Kweli's album "Life Is A Beautiful Struggle" and the struggles that come with breathing.

Life
Is one big beautiful struggle
That leads an adolescent to occupy the urban jungle and hustle
That inspired Mahatma Ghandi to starve
Encourages the full blown aids victim to wake up
It's in every land fertilizing the soil
Everywhere in the air
Breathe it
Even the blind man can see it
As if it leaves the leaves from the trees
Straight to our lungs
Filtered into our bones
All in our souls
It is what makes the baby escape the gates of the womb
That won't let Mumia lose hope
It is pain
It hurts
It is love
It's peace
It's in the prisoner's brain when he runs the yard
And keeps the sympathetic guards with the rifle in the gun
        towers reporting to their job
Families must be fed
Struggle!
Just can't escape it
It's on every corner
On every block

In every house
In every jail
From cell to cell
As high as the entities in the sky
As low as the unknown which inhabits the ocean's floor
It's swinging on the pole with the strippers chasing tuition
It is in the ink of the author scripting the suicide note
It guides the chalk of the underpaid public school teacher
It just won't let the conscious ones stop reaching out
      to the ignorant
And with all of its tears and blood
Busted arteries
Grey hairs
And burials
It is BEAUTIFUL...

The Poets

A poem about the poets.

What separates the poets from the rest of humanity is how they
    express their inner voice and visions
When the rest of mankind strangles their inspiration due to their
    fear of criticism or just mere laziness
The poets capture the zillions of thoughts floating amongst the
    ethers and proclaim the revelations without worry of
    reproach
The poets comprehend the language of the beast
The speech of the insects
And the dialect of the fowls flight in the sky
The poets communicate with all of the earth's planets
Translates for the stars
Where the people only see the cemented structure of the Great
    Wall in China
The poets speak for the peasant workers who died while they
    exhaustedly labored constructing the phenomenon and
    were buried inside of its concrete and graves became a
    supporting foundation for the great wonder of the world
The poets hear the trees weep for the bodies that were lynched
    and set ablaze savagely amongst its branches
The poets consoles the soil of Asia when it cries for justice for
    being defiled by orange agents and atomic solutions
The poets shut out the world to open up the universe within
And explain your thoughts while manipulating your senses...

Set Up

A verse from a song that I wrote with my comrade Daru about the challenges that await the Afrikan descent people in Amerikkka.

Whether I'm manifesting or studying my lessons
Been in the presence of oppression since I was adolescent
The question is how they got us believing we were born heathen
Since perfection in the semen I was born grieving
For all the wrong reasons got us dreaming we all leaving
Never perceiving they deceiving in the form of treason
In tune with my uniqueness like white sand on beaches
The pyramids in Egypt the virgin birth and 'Esa
Cradle to grave plantation field to cage
Cotton picking to prison burning crosses and lynching
It was already written aint nothing new under the sun
Under the gun like Malcom's only begotten son
Shed my blood to show that loves not pain
Stop sending our kids to public schools they
        bleaching their brain
Legs wide open in church man the preacher then came
Loyalty is lost in the communities the streets aint the same
Keep your third eye open destruction is coming
AIDS, breast cancer birth control pills is destroying our women
Now I know why they call where we live the projects
Use to test diseases on lab mice now hoodrats
Nobody left the womb pursuing Buicks and Uzis
Sublimely suggested to me by bad music and movies
Once I realized that we wasn't meant to survive

Whether you in college working for a law firm or just doing time
Incarcerated in the flesh my vision is prison
Signs and symbols is for the conscious mind this is beyond
        wisdom
Babylon is falling I know their time is up
I'm fed up I got to keep my head up it's a set up!

Chain of Thoughts

This was written after I read the biography of Johnny Spain. After reading about his personal horrific experience with chains (ankle shackles, belly chains, and handcuffs), I was able to recognize the psychological damage that I have suffered from them.

RUN!
Kunta Kinte
TOBY!
Get in those
CHAINS
Plantation
CHAINS
They sure would have loved to get Harriet in those
CHAINS
It's a crying shame what they did to Johnny Spain with those
CHAINS
Slave
CHAINS
CHAIN Gangs
Will the Afrikan descent male ever escape those
CHAINS
RUN!
No need for Harriet now
Can't escape those chains when they are on your brain
They sure would love to get Assata in those
CHAINS
You would think we have an aphrodisiac for these
CHAINS
Or the master and his descendants have a fetish for keeping us in
   those

CHAINS
The forecast looks the same
Heavy precipitation (tear drops)
And
CHAINS!

Black Body Swinging

When I was a child my grandfather sat me down and taught me about the meaning of Billie Holiday's song "Strange Fruit" and showed me the movie about her life titled "Lady Sings the Blues". Her song inspired me to write about the current state of our people.

I am the feeling that haunted Billie Holiday when she saw that
      black body swinging from a tree
So symbolic isn't it?
Our people hanging in thin air
At first the hanging man struggles for his existence
Pulling at the rope
Fighting for a chance to breathe
Brown vs.The Board of Education
Civil rights bill
Affirmative action
Muhammad Ali
Jackie Robinson
Althea Gibson
Paul Robeson
Josephine Baker
Fighting to breathe
Clawing at the rope around their necks
But now
Sad to say
The lynching is complete
The legs are no longer kicking and the rigor mortis has set in
No more Attica riots or Soledad Brothers
Replaced our Malcom and Martin for misinformed entertainers
Who will die for the task of our enlightenment?
Not the thespians, performers, and ball handlers

Too comfortable with their million dollar contracts and cozy in
    their secluded mansions
Sort of like seeking guidance from Sambo and casting off Nat
    Turner as delirious
Not even the tree can give oxygen to this lifeless body
Billie
What you saw stayed with you a lifetime
But I see your nightmare every moment that my eyes possess
    sight
The black body don't even swing no more
It's just hanging...

Lay Him Down Easy

I wrote this for a brother's (Malik) nephew who was murdered over a ten dollar debt and argument. Isn't life worth more?

Nothing but hate and ignorance in his veins momentarily insane
Unaware of from which it came until the body was slain
So childish we call this reckless style of living the game
Just to satisfy our pride we put our families in pain
Cause only one dies but both families are visiting graves
The cemetery and the murderer that remains in chains
And the government don't care to them it's two in one
And less welfare assistance for our future urban daughters
    and sons
Close our general hospitals and every time somebody
    is shot in a killing
The cops watch over top and leave the concrete to heal him
And if you can't afford a funeral you got to cremate him
Plus still pay taxes for the shooter while he is incarcerated
Somebody's aunt, somebody's uncle, somebody's niece,
    somebody's nephew
Didn't make it through the last night that we slept through
Man ain't it sad how the grim reaper crept through
With no words of condolence only with tears that he left you
Why do you have to sneeze just for somebody to bless you
Our communities are in a state of emergency and in need of a
    rescue
How is it that we aint at war and it's more black women
"Burying their children more than Iraqi women."
How many people today at a funeral like us
Cause their loved one died behind that federal note that says
    "In God We Trust"

As soon as you leave the funeral parlor another family enters
        and grieves just like you
And we all questioning destiny thinking he died before his time
Some of us have lust of revenge on our minds
Black mother I apologize for all of my misguided Black brothers'
        crimes
Instead of vengeance we have to unite our minds to break the
        soul eating cycle in these
Perilous times…

Regular Joe

This was written about a brother named Joe A.K.A Folks, that was held captive with me at D.C. Jail when we were teenagers. Meeting him now again almost eight years later, I realized that some brothers who were captured at the age of sixteen and given life sentences still remain adolescent inside, even though they are now approaching their mid-twenties. It is sad and scary at the same time. It feels "strange" to watch grown males with thick beards and mustaches, portray dominant juvenile characteristics. These caged graves have "stagnated" them.

For he came to this world
This cold world of cemented demons and chains
For he entered a child
A man-child
A child of circumstance
A child of violence
Of his environment
He was casted to a dungeon
He knelt upon his knee in prayer
With all his wild child crimes and sins weighing down upon him
He sent a divine petition to his lord
Demanding an "Immediate" release from captivity
Only to receive in return
A life sentence and a closed steel door
An officer waiting outside of his grave
Armed to the teeth with a sinister grin
And the intention to shatter even his intimate dreams
        of liberation
So Joe has put his middle finger up at the heavens
To curse the god that he once thought existed

Joe is confused
For he thinks that love is hate
Love is stupid
But yet he sees no extremes to his search for love
Joe is confused
Consumed in this cold world
This planet of hate
In a prison of snakes
Where love is fake
So he believes love is hate
You cannot blame him
For he has never seen man allow love to escape no further than
      the borders of his tongue
Joe is confused
Or maybe not
Can you challenge his belief that in Man Love is a Myth?

Black Sister

A spin-off to Angie Stone's "Black Brother" song.

We need to rep and protect them
Instead of sex and neglect them
And how you expect to respect them
When you steady sexin' their rectum
I love the women in college, the one with knowledge in prison
Who made the decision to travel with eighty bricks of that izm
And who wasn't flinching when feds asked to frisk them
Lost their kids, a life sentence, and still wasn't snitching
So in light of these facts how you gone call them bitches
When they be toting the pack in balloons in rooms on visits
Black Queen Black Diva I'll never leave you
Claiming the messed up ones like Star Jones and Condeleeza
The big-boned conscious sisters like Jill Scott and Queen Latifah
The girls in the hood plotting to set it off on the roof smoking
    reefer
Sophisticated ladies who listen to the jazz and blast the grass
To all the Coretta Scott Kings' and Betty Shabazzs'
You so fantastic young single mothers the task was drastic
Raising a male bastard whose father was dead or locked up in a
    casket
They was on the slave ship with us, the plantation with us
Burnt crosses in our lawns they ran out front doors with gauges
    with us
They stayed with us
Government incarcerated us media labeled us as thugs they still
    favored us
I wrote this for the teachers and mothers at PTA meetings
And I aint gave up on the ones in the strip club freaking

Peace to the young Tyra Banks at photo shoots in Africa to Nova
    Scotia
But I think we need more Sista Souljahs
Survived the crime ridden poverty stricken and hard living
But every Christmas and thanksgiving you kept giving
So this day let it be said
That all that calling you pigeon and chicken heads is officially
    dead…

Woman-Child

I wrote this about my little cousin Zenobia who has experienced foster homes, adoption, correctional facilities, residential homes and much more in her fourteen years of living.

Mother never cared
Father wasn't there
Filled with hate
Wanting love
She is naked in a cold world
With no family to keep her warm
No umbrella to protect her from the storm
So the tears of the heavens rain on her parade
No sun to brighten her days
Why does she have to sink so low just to get high
Feeling like making it to tomorrow is so hard so why should she
    try
When today makes her cry and love to die
Looking for a reason to smile
Hoping that it will get better in a while
Woman-Child…

Tanesha

I wrote this about a friend who loves her children's father deeply but only receives hurt and pain in return for her sincere dedication to him.

All she knows is love
She does not know how to fake it
But misunderstood that opening her legs was not how to make it
You can't make love my love
He beats her and leaves her
Grieves her and cheats her
Somehow she thinks she needs him
She made love
He made lust
Upon this commotion
A child is conceived when they both close their eyes and bust
She dreams of the big beautiful wedding festivities and happy
        family
He sees that she is getting fat
The attraction is gone
The lust is lost
"I don't love you!" He screams at her
She swears she hates him
Then starts to ask herself what did she do wrong
She blames herself then tells him that she needs him
Legs are reopened
Another conception
Her dream vanishes
The cycle perpetuates
She could not see hate even if it was branded on his face...

April

A brother showed me a picture of a sister I graduated from junior high school with. I was shocked because she had on excessive make-up, cups of liquor in her hand, looked aged and her smile seemed coerced. Her aura screamed sadness. During my eight years of imprisonment, I kept a youthful image of her in my mental rolodex. I sometimes forget that I left society at the age of sixteen and that people who I grew up with do not look the same anymore. The brother told me about how the sister had got on drugs, started having sex with females, and attempted suicide. I named this poem after her.

Who are you?
Where are you?
You!
You who I once knew
What happened to you?
You!
You who used to smile a lot before your days turned blue
You!
You who used to be so full of life
Now my words are heard inside echoing inside the hollowness
        of your soul
How did you become so empty?
You!
You before the make-up and ecstacy
When did you start thirsting for sour grapes?
You!
Your waters were innocent
When did you become so dry?
What incited you to get drunk?
Who murdered you?

What killed you?
You!
You before your smiles appeared forced
You who laughed naturally for your days
Before you wanted to commit suicide to avoid facing your
      tomorrow
You were so cute
You was so fresh
I had a crush on you
Before you crushed that part of you
You!
You who I once knew
You who was sexy without having sex or taking off your clothes
You!
This new you
I respect you
But if you run across that old you
Young you
You!
You who I once knew
Tell you that I miss you
Love You!

All Grown Up

A brother showed me some pictures of a sister that I graduated from junior high school with (not April, another sister). He informed me that she had 2 children and was selling herself on the internet. I got the pictures and sent them back to her with a letter of encouragement. I wrote this poem as I looked at her pictures.

You are so precious
You deserve to be shielded and protected
Seems like yesterday was 10 years ago in junior high when we
      received our diplomas on stage
Now you're a mother of two and I lay confined in this cage
You were the cute chinky eyed girl that always kept a smile
And I communicate with your soul through your eyes in these
      pictures and understand that life has not afforded you that
      sincerely in a while
Though some may view your auction of your image and
      physique as a misguided act of vain
But even though I am restrained with these shackles and chains
I drown my heart with tears because I truly feel your pain
I apologize for all of the males who have treated you
      with disrespect
I have grown to view all of you sisters with the honor I
      naturally gave my mother and to treat you as a queen and
      nothing less
Something is wrong you should not have to resort to this to
      sustain the clan
When will the grown boys stop playing games, being players,
      and get serious about being a man?

Whose Beauty

A poem inspired by a woman who is determined to get breast implants.

Somebody convinced you that you are ugly
Sent you to the good book for self-upliftment
Society has robbed you of your true worth
Got you judging yourself off of superficial standards
Going to run to put jelly in your chest
And think aint nobody going to see the vanity in your heart
Been passed by for so many high yellow and pale passions
That you secretly believe that your beauty is lacking
Hard to comprehend that I want you just the way you are
And that I see the beauty in the stretches of birth that you view
　　as a scar
Don't tell me that you desire the cosmetic butchery to please
　　yourself
When we know that you really just want to feel beautiful in the
　　eyes of someone else…

S-N-L

A brother asked me to write a poem about Sincerity and Loyalty. I wrote this for him but it was inspired by the bond and love of Ossie Davis and Ruby Dee.

Isn't it reasonable that I ask not for perfection?
Only sincerity and loyalty
Could love truly sustain without the elements of sincerity?
For what is love without sincerity but an empty noun that dwells
      on the tongues of many
Is not love in reality a verb?
Actions and movements
Not reduced to four letters that merely await in the unknown
It is not a spook
It is known
It is strong like the marrow that stiffens the bones
It is never alone
But always amidst many expressions dying to be shown
It is loyal
You cannot "make it" amongst five minutes of pleasure
You do not "fall in" it like a trap
You do not "fall out" of it
It will die for you
It will live for you
It is beyond egotism
Purged of materialism
It has no place for pride
There at your worst of times
Humble with you at your zenith
And most beautiful of all
It is consistent

With sincerity and loyalty
We experience the unexplainable…

She Loves Me

The many empty I LOVE/ MISS YOU'S that I have received from sisters.

She said that she missed me
But I never saw her
She wondered how I had grown
But never came to see me
She told my father that she had not heard from me in a while
But she never accepted my calls
She said she was jealous and possessive of me
But shared me in this cage with loneliness and her sister
     depression
But she told me she would never participate in ménage á trois
She said that she cared for me
But rarely wrote me
So I thought that for short notes she didn't care
She told me that when I come home that I would leave her
But when I searched for her in my captivity she was never there
Best of all she told me that she loved me
Worst of all I believed her
She told me she loved me
She told me she loved me
I truly believe her
She just has bad habits of showing me…

Love

It's about Love. —

Love
Oh how sweet I have never grown tired of thee
Seems like the world have forgotten you but me
Love
When or where did we lose you
Who fooled us to think we could live without you
Love
Why do we teach our children to read, write,
        and spell before thee
How could we abandon to learn the gift of your science
Love
Do you have a color
Seems as if these days you are blue
Is this new?
Did it ever exist a moment that you were bright
        that we once knew
Could it be true?
Love
You are one of the few things that money still can't buy
Seems like everyone's loyalty has its price but you
Love
Who decided to give you a name
Too big for four letters to contain
Only You even a genius find hard to explain
Love
Am I silly out of my mind
For trying to find you even when it feels as if you are extinct in
        these times

Love
My interest in you has become an obsession
For I desire your lessons
And cherish you presence
Love
Do not remain imprisoned to my tongue
Filter the blood in my veins
Encase my heart
To you I surrender my brain
Embrace my pain
Guide my every step along my journey of life
Precede my words
Cleanse my thoughts
Do not let my hands reach to touch without you
Let me breathe you
I need you
Love
Because of you I could not testify on the stand
Against my best man
So I take my captivity head up with no doubts strong like a man
Love
Allow me your intimacies
Let me procreate with you
Heal this sick world from hate with you
I would hate to be fake with you
I'll be faithful
Love
You are necessary food for the soul
Why do so many people abstain from you?
The people are starving for your attention
Famished hearts suffer hunger pangs when you are mentioned
Love
Without you the walls of sympathy inside of the people are dry
I guess that is why so many babies die and we can't cry
Love

By you I'm affected
And I have trouble resting at night
When I know that millions of my loved ones are in Africa HIV
    infected
Love
Can I taste your sweets
Wash and kiss your feet
For I've been OUT too long
I want to be IN you
In
In You
In those feelings that bring peace
Those thoughts that force smiles and destroy tension
That lends wings and allows me to see in other dimensions
Love
How come everyone wants to attain you
But can't explain you
Love!?

Loves Worth

Silly me! Trying to explain the worth of a jewel that is priceless. Or is it really like so? How much does yours cost? Don't be cheap because it might be fake.

LOVE
When it is real
Commands loyal allegiance
Lifetime dedication
Has no fear of commitment
Is worthy of eternity
Patient for its maintenance
Passion for it's satisfaction
Salaciously unified
Beautifully multiplied
A village of Love
A dynasty of peace
LOVE
When it is sincere
Deserves attention
Appreciation
Honorable mention
Divine conviction
A fight not to lose it
Tears when it seems lost
Because
LOVE
When it is true
It's suppose to last till the end of time
Till the sun no longer shines
Because it sometimes takes forever to find

And when it is gone
Can make you lose your mind
So
LOVE
When it is valued at it's worth
Hold it
Mold it
Fashion it for your soul to mate and grow old with...

I Beleive in Love

My faith in Love.

I believe in Love
I believe that Love transcends bars, walls, air, hearts, hate
I believe in Love
I believe that Love is the root of all righteous causes
The cause behind all movements
The spark that ignites all revolutions
The fuel that blazes the torch of past struggles
That incites the present to grasp it and keep the flames ablaze
I believe in Love
And in faith and patience
But of these three
Love reigns supreme
I believe in Love
I believe Love works
I believe in Love
That Love is real
Love never fails
I believe in Love…

Much Love

All of the many faces of love.

Old Love
Young Love
That Brian McKnight she gives me crazy Love
Beyonce's dangerously in love
Making Love
I hate you Love
Make-up Love
Thug Love
All day Love
All night Love
Tony Montana Love
John Coltrane love supreme Love
Groupie Love
That chicken soup, crackers, and ginger ale nurse me back to
        health Love
Musiq Soulchild Love
Puppy Love
Love your enemy Love
Love should have brought you ass home last night Love
Aint nuthin' like that mother Love
Bobby and Whitney Love
Ossie Davis and Ruby Dee Love
Grandma Love
I can't wait to get home Love
Just can't wait to get to the bedroom in the kitchen Love
Rip the cloths off Love
I could not live to see you with another Love
Confused Love

In denial Love
Travel the distance and visit prison Love
No boundary Love
Unconditional Love
Can't live without you Love
Fiftieth wedding anniversary Love
The Mya head over heals I'm fallen for you Love
The Alicia Keys in and out Love
If all this is Love
Then what is Love
One Love!!!

Questioning Love

A few questions for loving self.

If I asked you did you love yourself
Would you tell me that you loved yourself
If I asked you how you loved yourself
Could you tell me how you loved yourself
If then you realized that you did not love yourself
Would you cry because you really want to love yourself
Maybe that would help you love yourself
Help to love
Loving to help others
Selfless love
Doesn't mean you have to love yourself less…

Can I

Can I love you with no limits or inhibitions?

Can I grab your ear?
Can I ease your fears?
Can I love you young?
Can I love you old?
Can I work the middle?
Can I kiss your toes?
And caress your soul
Can I be all that you need?
Can I be more than a king?
Can I be too good to be true?
Plus more than a dream
If skies are the limit
Can we go beyond the limit of the sky?
Can I make your day?
Can I make you cry?
Tears of joy
Can I cool your eyes?
When your heart is with pain
If love lends wings
Can make you fly?
Can I take you high?
Can I make you believe?
This is more than a dream
This is You and Me…

What I Need

The encircle and pull factor toward my Queen. Circling her with
spectacular demands and pulling her to perfection.

Like Aaliyah I want you to be more than a woman
Sort of like Nefertiti but more than a queen
A young Betty Shabazz and Coretta Scott King
I'm trying to graduate you from the class of Reebok and tight
    jeans
The way that I feel is more real than a dream
I crave for you more like a fiend
Never limit my vision just to us having children
I'm thinking you and me old gray with wrinkles and
    grandchildren
You've always been dear to me
I want you here with me
When I die get buried beside me
I want you near to me

A Love We Once Knew

A poem inspired by an ancient love that seems unrealistic in these loveless times.

Ancient Kimetics didn't have one word for love
Just an expression manifested by ebony complexions
More than opposite sexes having sex with the sexes
Sort of spiritual affection that was divinely directed
There was no need for protection
We did not have disease
Back then females were queens
No sluts and skeezers...

Salacious Solitude

Surrounded by a complete darkness that invades us as if an
     earthquake has temporarily relieved the entire planet from
     its electricity
Amidst a moment of complete isolation that confines us at the
     time that rests even the occasional rodent or insect that
     may intrude the most hidden privacies
Only to be witnessed by the illumination that burns from the
     incense and candles that is amongst our presence
I place my nose along the very strands of the texture of your
     hairs to overdose my nostrils with the scent of your scalp
I hold your face between the palms of my hands and imprison
     my eyes to your stare
In silence
I watch you
Allowing our pupils to converse in a clearly understood
     unspoken language of a million words
After our lips embrace
We become totally engrossed with tasting each other's enamel
And setting our tongues out on a crusade to conquer one
     another tonsils
Then I nibble on your ear and lick every carved crevice within it
Slowly I ease my way down vampire like upon your neck as you
     tilt your head to the side and moan
I admire the artistry of the painting of your areola as I encircle its
     perfect outlining with my tongue
Then with my saliva I gently massage the stiffness of your tips
I creep slowly to drink the sweet waters of your valley as my
     hands pull aside the grass amongst the shore
I handle you with the firmness of a man
But lick, suck, touch, and explore you with the skilled precision
     of a lesbian who has fulfilled the curiosities of many

women
I penetrate many inches within your shallow waters with rapid
but smooth adrenaline that causes a convulsion like a
typhoon within the surface of your soul
Then sit with you naked as we feed each other fresh fruits and
recite freestyle poetry to one another
Completely naked
No clothes
No lies
No suspicions
No doubts
No fears
No egos
No pretensions
No tension
No self-consciousness of what the world may perceive as
physical flaws
No distractions
No hurry
No sense of time
No rules
No worries
Just a magnanimous moment

I'm Weak

The battle which rages within the heart of every righteous man.

I fast
I read
I pray
I struggle
I lower my gaze
Those lips and hips
That flesh erect from the bones of the chest called breast
I'm weak!
I see it
I look away
I hear it
Then plug my ears
I smell it
I cover my nose
It's in my mind spreading like a wild untamed ferocious fatal
        forest fire
This is too much for one heart to extinguish
I'm weak!
I don't like it
Sometimes say I hate it
Too temperamental
Scary emotional
Even called it evil
But
I want it
Sometimes I say I need it
I love it
I'm weak!

I give up
The resistance and struggle
Desiring it is too natural
Like breathing
Its pull is inevitable
Like death
Hips and lips
Flesh erect from the bones of its chest called breast
I'm weak!

Thank You Note

Showing my appreciation for all those sisters (who I love soooooo much) who wrote their thoughts during my struggle. Much love. A young warrior needed that in his battle to survive in these insane asylums.

I just thought I'd thank you for every letter you wrote
On them days I thought I wouldn't be able to cope
Some days I thought it would be best just to hang from a rope
But I read your words and you just gave me hope
Locked up in a cage for 23 hours a day
Only to go outside and see the sun through a cage
My skin turned pale thinking I'd die in jail
Feeling alive in of a coffin and my cell was hell
Sometimes I got impatient and thought you aint love me no
        more
Until the C.O. walked past and dropped your note on my door
I'd smell your letter an fall back on my bed
Close my eyes with thoughts of sucking your neck and your
        breast in my head
Put my headphones on and listen to Brian McKnight
Felt like I was going on a date when I would write you a kite
Inspired me to work and study the law
And stay focused on what awaits me on the other side of this
        door…

For So Long

We have been struggling for so long.

We have been shackled and chained up for so long
Been whipped and name changed for so long
Since master Willie Lynch we have been colliding against each
    other for so long
The skin complexions, gangs, and religions aint going to divide
    us but for so long
Burnt crosses on our lawn for so long
But we aint going to hold on but for so long
Cops shooting us down unarmed for so long
We aint going to forgive the bombings of black Wall Street in
    Tulsa and Move in Philly but for so long
We aint going to accept having the worst public schools and you
    still closing them down but for so long
We been fighting in your wars for so long
To come home and have police beat us in the street for so long
We can't be dumb for so long
And accept your crack laws and getting tough on crime
    politicians wishes but for so long
We've been singing we shall overcome for so long
Slavery, Brown vs. the Board of Education, Affirmative Action,
    Civil Rights Act for so long
Jim Crow and Rockerfeller Laws how do you expect us not to
    fight back for so long
You've miscalculated us for so long
Native Americans, Jews, Japanese, and how do you expect us not
    to demand reparations for so long

You then wronged us for so long
Nat Turner, Johnathan Jackson, John Brown, George Jackson,
        Steve Bingham showed you
misjudged us for so long…

Keep On Pushing

An encouragement for people to move forward with the burdens that accompany life.

Life is full of obstacles
Remove one to have another one on top of you
Soon as you make it halfway amidst a worrisome struggle
Two more unbearable barriers are cemented in front of you
But the impossible we must bear
And barriers remain barriers as long as we ALLOW them to
      remain there
Remember Aunt Assata said "A wall is a wall and nothing more
      at all"
Berlin is a sign that fortress can fall
So we can't afford to be weak and only complain when we are
      captured in chains
Study the curriculum of Grandma Harriet because the objective
      is the same

Problems

A brief illustration of some of the many mental diseases that ails brothers.

Black Entertainment Television got us all gone
That we can't see the value of women ouside of a thong
Instead of teaching our children how to count, read and spell
We got the baby mother putting up the house for our bail
Can't stay out of jail and as far as I can tell
We only use them for visits, money orders, and some mail
Hit the streets and don't practice nothing we preach
Leave the people thinking all prisoners' intensions are weak
And I can't blame them all them promises convicts then gave
     them
Feeling like only ecstasy and Remy Martin can save them...

Objectivity

A plea to the people's conciousness of what's really happening around them.

After 9/11 the reward for your patriot acts
Signed you a bill
Legislated to make society a reflection of a supermax
Surveillance from the stars
Credit cards, checks, and receipts leave a trail
Not even library books and groceries are private when they are
     investigating every sale
Sending your kids to foreign lands to die for pre-emptive
     suggestions
Look at your crusades for civilizing and colonizing if you want
     to locate destructive weapons
Spending billions of dollars on NASA to search the heavens for
     objects extraordinary and special
When everything about your consistency to create chaos is
     Extra-Terrestrial!

Imagine That

Originally a song that I wrote about the possibilities of the world.

Imagine that the sky was black
And lies were facts
You didn't have to rhyme with raps
There would be no rhythm
No religion
No sinning
And Brooklyn brung the Dodgers back
And women went for conscious cats doing life in prison
Imagine that life was sacred and respected
Women could walk the street naked and still feel protected
Imagine that every morning in bed your queen bought you
       breakfast
And life was so precious that we all felt breathless
Imagine that the youth wasn't reckless with a death wish
You could walk every city in America without weapons
Imagine that you had sex with no liquid ejaculations
And babies were created by thoughts and imaginations
Then we would all be creative
Working both sides of our brains because that's the way our
       creator made us

Superwoman

Black Mama!

You told me that I was a painless labor
My delivery was swift
You told me that strangely I did not cry when I escaped your
        womb
Even when the doctor smacked me on my behind
I still did not utter a shout
A silent birth
Unusual you figured at that time
Maybe the lack of pains and screams
Was a retribution for all the suffering I brought your heart
The many tears that my existence has cost you
But you still loved me
Through all the fights at school and suspensions
The truancy hearings and insolence
The court dates
Seeing me chained like a slave
The shelter houses, probation, jails, prisons, and penitentiaries
You never stopped loving me
The lockdowns, stabbings, and years of solitary confinement
Losing my visits
Losing my phone
Losing my mind
You loved me harder
It's no wonder when the world condemned me
You never lost hope
Never stopped giving
Loving
The saddest thing is that

Even though I know that you are a superwoman
I feel ashamed to admit that
I've been your worst kryptonite

Free

Allah said there is no harm in repaying an injury for an injury
equally for what is received
But he said it is best to be patient and forgive
Muhammad (SAW) said that the strongest man is not the person
who can carry the heaviest weight but the one who can
forgive when they are angry
Solomon (AS) said that the patient man is better than the
warrior and he who can control his temper rather than one
who takes a city
Jesus (AS) told the disciples to love their enemies
I now understand
I AM FREE

Energy

The source and force which is with the righteous struggle.

Literally
I can't be seen with the mysterious eyes
I travel the speed of generations
I enter shells as smooth as air
Not even the soul notices that I am there
I've reformed beast into men
And mere men into machines
Where there is darkness
I bring light
I've turned vile prisoners into princes' for the people
By me
The peasants have rebelled
And struck the death blow to anarchy
I taught the slaves how to read
They thought they destroyed me by hanging John Brown in
    Harper's Ferry
But I showed my face in Stephen Bingham
My patterns are too abstract for psychoanalysts to grasp
I am color blind
Truth and justice are my kind
I free the minds from mental swine
Then seize the time
As I unify the blind
When my presence is near
I scare off the fear
That devilishly lingers
I'm a righteous bringer
I bleed ink on pages

I seduce the sages
I am waiting between the covers
For the liberation of lovers
I conquer conscious
And move with movements
Visit jails
And bring heaven to hells
See what I did to Malcolm Little
Everything grows from a cell…

Message From The Author

First of all, I thank Allah for giving me life and good health. With those two blessings all things are possible. Thank You!

In my first book (A Reason To Breathe) I did not name everybody within my struggle by name, and some people, especially the hood, wasn't feeling that. So, this is my attempt to give all of you, your proper place in history.

Queen Darlene (My mother and dearest love). I love you super-woman, black mama give me my kiss! Jesse Devil (My father). Nobody said a father is supposed to be perfect. I appreciate your presence.

To Angela Stewart: you deserve your own chapter in my heart. I apologize for falling in love with you, but nobody puts up with my shit like you. What we have is bigger than love. I trust you! Tell your mother she's great. She made you.

To the future president of S.A.T.O. Daru Swinton. Hey Handsome! My brother from another mother. We can never replace all those talks on the bench in the yard. I'm just setting all of this up for you! I'm in debt to you forever. You showed me how to put that charisma with my militancy. Now I'm just too crazy, sexy, and cool.

Momolu, Kareem, Ali, Jesse, Chip, and Zay. The original team. We go back like throwing nerf footballs in Azeeze Bates Alley and sleeping in the same bed. Memories too rich to be erased! If your name wasn't mentioned in this paragraph (you know who you are) it was very intentional you get the picture.

Jabril (lil' brother), Chip (big sis), Pup, Mema, Donny, Charles, Martina, Tay, Aunt Ruth (favorite, your always you, consistent), Moe, Pooda, Tarshia (Mrs. Shorter), June Bug, Mondez (holla at your lil' peoples, thanks for making me tough), Tiffany, Shawn and Chrissy, Aunt Landa, Mimi and Ree Ree (might have spelled it wrong but you know who you are), Monica Kendra, Tanesha, Crewall (sorry if I misspelled), Aunt Sadie, Frankie, Jameelah, Tova, Kendra, King, Kevin, Davina, Kiesha and Quita, Mrs. McCraney, Ms. Lynn, Ms Kim, Ms Sheryl, Nikki, Ms. Naimah, Ms. Bell, Ms. Stanley, Tutu (Fatu) and Ms. Stewart, Kendia ('Aleemah my sister) get that degree and introduce West Liberty College to you brothers books , Quanda, Rhonda, Wanda, Shanda, Candyman, Junior, Poopi, Ron, Jay, Zenobia, Tyrek, Lil' Anthony, Bobby, Quinn, Iran, Asia, Japan, Zandi, Auntie Girl, Aunt Pat, Donte, Mrs. Pulliam for raising a good son, Billy for holding Daru down, Chris, Derek, Myron Briggs, Ricky, Timmy, Uncle Elijah, Aunt May, Marylyn and Walter and their kids, Ms. Joanne, Marlon, and Ageel.

To my stepmother Katrina who I think is a solid black woman.

To my cousin Boo aka Sultan. The eccentric poet. Go to Amazon.com and cop his first book.

To my niece, Kanier "Armani" Shorter, My Heart. I'm writing so that I can spoil you rotten. (I don't like those tight jeans)

Ashanti, my grandfather who taught me all that good black Harlem Renaissance Jack Johnson, Joe Louis, Charlie Parker, and Billie Holiday history. I got you to out of here before you go.

To queen Anissa, I was never writing poetry until I met you. Growing Pains, Confessions of Concious Hearts by Anissa Chisley and Halim Flowers coming soon. I feel honored to share pages with my poetic oracle.

To my mentor in this struggle "Minkah" aka Michael Norwood, the man who showed me business, class, and professionalism. Go to Amazon.com and purchase his books "I'm Not Crying" and "Looking For a Way Out". Another brother behind these walls writing books.

To Eyonne Williams, another brother locked down penning classics. Go to Fastlane.com and support the brother with his book "Fastlane". Tyrone Hines, another prison writer who wrote "Wanted By The Feds" and "Drugs, Money and Violence". Support the brother. To my comrade Jay who is about to release a trilogy. The first book "Can You Stand The Rain"is coming soon. Eric VanBuren who will have his book "Double Life" out soon. Also big Shaka who has the new best seller on relationships coming out soon. Plus Panama aka Jamie Davidson. Go to his website on friendsbeyondthewall.com and support his legal struggle. Raymond Ramirez, who will be the top writer for S.A.T.O. soon, you're the chosen one.

To my protégé Tyesheauana Wright. Tye-Tye. Hope, for the future. Keep writing.

To my comrades behind the wall: C-Dog, Nut , Butchie, Champ, Big

George (genuine brother), Ageel, Hasaan (who read it all before it hit the press), Lil Marvin, D.C., Folks, C-Murder, Dirty (Luther Fuller) and all the brothers from the juvenile block with me. Black (Pittsburgh), Lil Jonesy (Buffalo). All the brothers who be up in the law library fighting for their freedom. Anybody else real, if I forgot your name it was not intentionally.

Muhaymin: who revived my deen and taught me real Islam. I don't know why you believed in me but you did.

To everybody from around the way. Maleekah (Pig), Shayla, Teresa, Karen, Dog, Big Geno, Brian. Forgive me if I forgot any names it's only been nine years.

Special thanks to the beautiful sister Shashonia. Thank you. I'm Sorry that the beginning of the book caused you to lose sleep when you were typing it. But, the struggle is beautiful and real like that. Don't worry; it doesn't make me weak or bitter. I'm getting stronger every oppressive moment.

In closing, I pray that the brothers out there step up and be fathers to their children and the sisters be good mothers. The foundation of our struggle starts in the home and like Bill Cosby said, we have to start being good parents. I encourage people to stop committing crimes so that we can put this billion dollar prison business out of business. To the people that consciously still commit crimes, if or when you get arrested, STOP SNITCHING! Do your own time and stop helping the government divide families?

The U.S. criminal system is not about "justice" or "rehabilitation" but about "**cooperation.**" Sammy the "BULL" Grevano admitted to killing nineteen people in the John Gotti case but because he testified for the government he received five years for his crimes. At the age of sixteen, I was charged with aiding and abetting one murder and received a sentence triple plus the number of years Sammy the "BULL" Grevano received. For me its worth noting, at the time of my arrest (age sixteen) the "Bull" had killed more people during his crime spree than the sixteen years I had lived but he goes home to catch another case. Foremost, in my case, the charges against the person the government said was the shooter were dismissed! Amerikan Justice!

Everybody who has a loved one behind these walls should continue to show love. A letter, a card, some flicks. Don't forget the struggle. Brothers locked down need to unite and stop separating and warring against each other over some petty geographical differences. Its real men from China to Compton, so stop the trivial tribalism. We are all in the same struggle.

Thanks to all of my supporters, and especially the ladies that support the struggle. Special thanks to my prosecutor and judge who were vessels Allah used to put me through the fire to serve a greater purpose. Honestly, I aint mad at you. And once again Bugah Butt I love you. You know who you are. In 2007, if Allah wills, my novel "It Must Be Love" and another poetry book "Till My Last Breath" will be published and released. Love is shown through movements. Love never fails. Organize and Improve.

P.S. They tried to bury ME ALIVE but they can't KILL ME!

Light,
Halim

2-2-06